Win New Customers

How to Attract, Connect, and Convert More
Prospects into Customers in 60 Days Using
Digital Marketing Strategies

Jean Ginzburg

JEAN GINZBURG

Table of Contents

Introduction 5

Chapter 1: I Don't Have the Time for Digital Marketing 15

Chapter 2: I Am Not Tech Savvy...23

Chapter 3: My Business is Different—I Don't Need Digital Marketing......29

Chapter 4: Developing Your Customer Profile (Customer Avatar) 33

Chapter 5: Product Offering Strategy 39

Chapter 6: Content Strategy 45

Chapter 7: Facebook Advertising 51

Chapter 8: Landing Pages...57

Chapter 9: Nurture Funnels/Marketing Automation................................63

Chapter 10: Retargeting 71

Next Steps 79

About the Author 81

JEAN GINZBURG

Introduction

Before I started my digital marketing agency, I failed. More than once. It was tough in the beginning. I didn't know much about business or how to run a business. I did know about the subjects of the businesses I was running, but knowing what I know now, at that time I was clueless.

In 2008, I started my foray into entrepreneurship while I still had a full-time job. I set up an e-commerce shopping site using the affiliate model to monetize. My sister and I created the venture as a way to honor companies who gave back to the community or were eco-friendly. We featured these businesses on our site. I had come from the affiliate background and knew a lot about the industry, but at that time it was a little late to set up an e-commerce site. There were thousands upon thousands of these types of sites and competition was fierce. I also didn't know anything about optimizing organic traffic at the time. So we got no hits on our site and the venture fizzled out since we weren't making any money.

I went back to my regular full-time job. Disappointed. But the entrepreneurial spirit didn't stay away. I created several other businesses—an email marketing business and a wild mushroom foraging venture (I know, crazy, but I am knowledgeable about wild mushrooms).

Again, these ventures didn't bring in the cash. I went back to my full-time job, disappointed again. But in retrospect I learned a valuable lesson about this phase in entrepreneurship. Most business owners don't mention this very often. Everyone always talks about the success and how much money they are making. But I bet most entrepreneurs had previous businesses that failed. And what I learned here is don't give up. The first time you try it, it might not work. But keep at it. Have patience. Keep moving forward and maybe the fifth or the tenth time will be a winner.

A few years later, I was working at a digital agency and I was fed up. Fed up with the politics and the inefficiencies. This was my turning point. I had wanted to create my own venture and go on my own for years and I felt like this was the time.

My transition into entrepreneurship was slow. In retrospect, I think it was for the best, but everyone has their own journeys. Some are thrust into the roller coaster that is entrepreneurship.

I quit my full-time job at the agency and started consulting for one client. It was almost like a full-time job, but I was a contractor instead of a full-time employee. As a contractor, I picked up a few nuggets of information for owning my own business. I had to set up my own company, pay my quarterly taxes and do my own bookkeeping.

After about six months of consulting for one client, I realized that this was not a sound strategy. What would happen if this client decided to move on and did not need my services anymore (which of course happened down the line)? It was a risky time for me. If something were to go down with this one client, I would be out of business. I started thinking, *I am sure there are more potential clients out there who needed my services*.

I started looking for new clients. My process was haphazard. There would be months of feast or months of famine. I might find a few clients in one month, but go without any new clients for several months. A few times I was on the verge of closing my business. Luckily, I was able to weather the storm, but it made me think how easily my business can be taken away from me. I never wanted to feel that way. That sinking feeling of whether I am going to be able to pay rent next month.

I had to find a better solution.

I was doing mostly channel marketing for my clients. I would work on paid media for one client and then social media for another client and then content strategy for another client.

At the same time, I was diving deep into more advanced digital marketing. And before I go further, let me define digital marketing. According to the Financial Times, it's defined as the marketing of products or services using digital channels to reach consumers. The key objective is to promote brands through various forms of digital media. Digital marketing extends beyond internet marketing to include channels that do not require the use of the internet. It includes mobile phones (both SMS and MMS), social media marketing, display advertising, search engine marketing, and any other form of digital media.

All of this was very insightful for me at the time as I read hundreds of articles and blog posts. I went through dozens of digital courses— everything from list building to Facebook ads to funnels. Took countless workshops. Went to conferences and joined masterminds and groups.

It was my Renaissance.

I concluded that all digital marketing is interconnected. I can't run Facebook ads without a funnel. And I can't create a funnel without a marketing automation system.

I started to piece all this information together. There was a lot to internalize. All these "gurus" were giving only bits and pieces. One was talking about Facebook ads, another about list building. It seemed like all these "systems" the "gurus" talked about were created in a vacuum. But digital marketing is interrelated.

Additionally, I added the customer to all of this. What are the customer's needs? How do they fit in?

I felt like I was putting together a puzzle. I was trying to find all the pieces and then put them in the right place.

I started testing out my theories with my own customer acquisition strategy for my business. If I add in content to my strategy, what does that do? If I use video instead of images for my Facebook ads, how does that affect my overall results?

After a couple of years testing and theorizing, I came up with a framework.

I started incorporating my framework into my clients' marketing programs. And it worked for them! We could bring in customers on auto-pilot with this framework.

This whole thing took me five years to master. With lots of trial and error. Dozens of mistakes. I have boiled it down now for you, without you having to go through the long, tiring, endless process and make the same mistakes I made.

I am going share how you can create the same framework for your business and start bringing in customers on auto-pilot in 60 days or less. And you don't have to be a digital marketing expert.

Does this sound like you?

You don't know where to begin. You are frustrated because you don't know all the strategies and tactics to grow your business. You are all over the place—starting one thing, finding that at first sight it might not be working and giving up. Then jumping to the next shiny thing and only to find that it too has failed. This is known in the community as "shiny object syndrome." You love your idea or product but you don't know how to use digital marketing as a channel for your business. You also feel overwhelmed at all the steps needed to take to get to the final destination and it makes you uneasy. And on top of all that, you are getting customers haphazardly. One month you might have a ton of customers, the next month it's crickets.

You have an amazing business and a solid product. And I know you want to get there! I know you want to feel successful.

You want to get to the point where you know what you need to do to create a strategy for your business. You understand how to execute on next steps. You don't feel like digital marketing makes your head hurt or is too complex and complicated. You understand all the main components of digital marketing and you know how to use each of the components and at which time. You see your business growing and are excited you've created a successful venture.

With this book, I can take you there! I can get you to where you WANT to be.

Who is this book for?

If you're an entrepreneur, startup or small business owner who wants to grow your business using digital marketing, technology and automation, and has challenges managing all the customers, platforms and employees because you don't have the business processes in place or you don't have the time to do it all, this book is for you. If you have trouble bringing in new paying customers on a regular and consistent basis, this is for you. If you're looking to grow your business and attract satisfied customers who find value in your products, this is for you. Customers who have made the decision to buy from you because they know, like and trust you and your company. You know, the ones you don't have to sell to because they already love your company and your brand. Customers who will give you their money!

Even if you are just getting started with your online marketing and don't know what to do or where to start.

If you have experienced the following, then you are in the right place.

Are you feeling overwhelmed?

Feeling like you are putting in the effort for your online marketing and not getting any results?

Feeling like you are posting content and you are screaming into a crowd but no one is listening?

Feeling as though you have spent hundreds or thousands of dollars on paid media and netted very little?

If you want to continue doing what you are doing, then please put this book down.

You have probably tried from one to dozens of books, courses and paid programs targeted to entrepreneurs. These courses typically lure entrepreneurs in with amazing results and stretched stories of how someone, somewhere has made thousands of dollars utilizing this one method that will make you rich.

This book is different. And do you know why?

Because this framework has been refined and perfected over five years. This isn't just a quick system that I set up. This is a framework that worked for my business AND my clients' businesses.

This book will create a streamlined, predictable method to bring in new customers every day. It will allow you to understand the concepts you need to know to grow your business.

This book goes through all the aspects of customer acquisition. You don't need to buy multiple books for how to create funnels or how to run Facebook ads. This book contains the guide on to how to find new customers.

This framework is a long-term investment in your business. This isn't about making a quick buck. If you want to invest in your business to have as your own for your revenue stream or to eventually sell, this formula I used to grow my clients' businesses from several thousand dollars per month to seven figures per year can help you do that.

Results

I want to share some of my results with you.

I have run Facebook ad campaigns bringing in under $1.40 per lead for prospects who have never heard of my client's brand at the time (what we in the digital marketing industry call "cold traffic".)

I have run Google Adwords campaigns with a 742% ROI.

The proof is in the pudding. These are just some example of how my digital marketing strategies have brought in revenue to my clients' businesses. I have grown some of my clients' businesses from six to seven figures. This allowed them to expand their product line, expand their workforce and serve more customers. It's been a very exciting experience for me and my team to see my clients flourish.

Why I wrote this book

Most entrepreneurs have a lot of ideas thrown at them and they don't know where to start or how best to execute, so they don't execute at all. This book walks you through the process of marketing your business, with all the strategies and tactics that you need. It's not confusing and not meant to be like all the other books where "gurus" throw random ideas out at you, for a strategy that worked for them, at one point years ago.

What you will learn

You will learn a framework of how to consistently and predictably find new customers for your business. I go over a few myths that new entrepreneurs have about digital marketing and about running your own business. I am going to address the topic of how

11

entrepreneurs never have the time to do digital marketing. And the one thing I would say to that is if you don't have the time to do marketing, then your business isn't thriving. Marketing is an ongoing, living, breathing part of your business that every entrepreneur needs to work on no matter the business.

I know there are a lot of you out there who haven't done digital marketing because of the technology. Technology can be scary but I will walk you through some steps that will melt your fears away.

I am sure many of you are saying, "Well my business is different, so how can this work for my business?" The one thing I can say is that EVERY business needs marketing. If you aren't doing marketing in your business, then your business isn't growing.

Then I will get into the actual framework I developed to help you get new customers on auto-pilot! I will first go over your ideal customer profile and how to find your perfect customer. The one that loves your products and who will give their money to you. Then I am going to discuss content to bring this customer into the fold. Next, I will review a product strategy on how to ascend your perfect customer through a funnel—starting off small (so you don't scare them away) to bigger and bigger offers. Once you have developed and tested these components, you will create some ads to find your ideal, perfect customer on Facebook. This will feed the funnel with consistent and predictable prospects that you will convert into paying customers using your content, offers and automated email campaigns. Here is the flow of the entire framework.

Win New Customers Framework

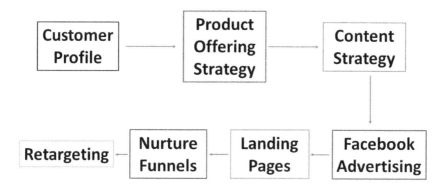

I also provide a 60 Day Digital Marketing Checklist (see Resources section at the end of this chapter) to walk you through the strategy and have a step-by-step process for you to follow as you create the digital marketing campaigns.

And to keep you motivated and taking action, at the end of each chapter I invite you for "Your Turn". This section gives you actionable next steps to implement the concepts, strategies and best practices to be executed in your business.

Additionally, I provide a Resources paragraph where you can find links to additional information, platforms and technologies.
Where applicable, I will include an analytics section to discuss benchmark analytics. Please keep in mind that every business is different and analytics might be different for your business, but these are benchmark analytics for general campaigns.

The key is consistency. Remember that marketing will require testing. One in five or one in ten ideas will work. But don't give up.

It takes the right audience, the right messaging, testing and hitting it on the nose in order to get the results and in order for someone to buy your product.

Now that we have covered who I am and my digital marketing framework, let's jump right into the details. The first thing I hear from entrepreneurs is, "Jean, I don't have the time to implement digital marketing in my business." So, our first step is to help you get back your time.

Resources

60 Day Digital Marketing Checklist — https://goo.gl/1C4TSD

Chapter 1: I Don't Have the Time for Digital Marketing

Every day you are hustling for your business. You feel like all you are doing is putting out fires. You respond to emails all day or help with a question for one of your employees, and then you look at your phone and you realize it's 4 p.m. and you haven't gotten any actual work done. All you have done is taken care of other people's needs. The sinking feeling is coming over you. You aren't working on the projects that are in truth bringing in revenue to your company.

I see this all the time. Entrepreneurs start businesses and get into the weeds. They start off helping customers and eventually learn that it's not just that, it's also running a business and doing the day-to-day activities to grow the business.

You feel like you are spinning your wheels all day long. You don't have the time to work on projects that drive revenue for your business. And you feel like your business is slipping away.

You are not alone. A lot of entrepreneurs feel this way.

But there is a solution: creating processes and systems to help you automate your business. I am sure there are many tasks you or your team do that are repetitious. The trick is to find how to automate these processes.

Imagine: you start your work day and there aren't fires. You get to your computer and review your sales reports to find that you exceeded your sales expectations for yesterday.

You call up one of your joint venture partners and set up a campaign to cross-promote your product on his list.

You feel like you are being productive and accomplishing what you need to drive and grow the business. You feel like you finally have time back.

In this chapter, I am going to show you the five systems that will get you time back to grow your business and demonstrate you how to automate the main processes of your business.

Systems to get back your time

#1: Standard Operating Procedure (SOP)

An SOP is a system of instructions using step by step procedures to help you or your team stay organized. Eventually you have tasks that you do every day. The easiest way to cut time and cut costs is to create a step by step process for these regular tasks.

SOPs cut down the time it takes to do each task, because you or your team don't need to think about how to do it every time. SOPs also cut down on training new people. You don't have to physically show each new employee how to do something, they can just review the process and understand how to do it.

Most businesses do not have SOPs. They rely on their employees performing these tasks. And that could be fine for now, but what if this employee leaves? Then no one in the organization knows how to complete this process.

Of course, it takes some time to create these processes and procedures. But in the long run it will save you a ton of time!

SOPs don't need to be fancy. I use a Google Sheet to create my processes. I have columns for the projects: login, videos, and step by step instructions. I use a screenshare video program called Jing to include instructions with visual demonstrations for my team on how to complete certain tasks. It's free and it allows you to create up to five-minute videos to go along with your instructions. After you create the video, the video is hosted on Jing's server and you can access it via a URL on your browser. So when I am performing a task, I use the screenshare video as I am going through the marketing platform – which page I visit, where I go, where I click, so my employees can follow along. Then I fill out the spreadsheet. I include the following key components:

- Login to the platform
- Link to Jing URL for step-by-step video
- Additional step-by-step written instructions

Keep all these instructions in your spreadsheet and share it with your team via Google Sheets. I include a sample Standard Operating Procedure in the Resources section at the end of this chapter.

There are also third-party platforms such as Sweetprocess that allow you to do the same thing but in a formal platform. While the Google Doc approach is easy to manage and does not require any costs, Sweetprocess is a more advanced platform that allows you to keep your procedures in one place. You can create a procedure, add in steps and videos and your whole team can have access to this platform. There is a link to Sweetprocess in the Resources section at the end of this chapter.

SOPs will save you tons of time and increase productivity for you and your team. I include a link to a sample Standard Operating Procedure in the Resources section at the end of this chapter. Refer back to your 60 Day Digital Marketing Checklist and create your Standard Operating Procedure in Days 1-7 (Week 1).

#2: Tech Integrations

We use a lot of technology platforms these days and reviewing the data and analytics for each platform is time consuming. Now you can integrate a lot of your platforms so data is streamlined.

For example, the e-commerce shopping cart platform, Shopify, does a very good job of integrating with third party platforms through their App Store (I have included a link to Shopify in the Resources section at the end of the chapter). This includes email platforms, social media, shipping, inventory, and accounting to name a few. Most of these integrations don't require you to be a coding genius. Just go into the platform, look for the Integrations tab and connect the platforms. While each platform might be different, you can always do a Google search of "how do I integrate X with Shopify".

For example, I have a Shopify client and I was able to easily integrate their Facebook Ads account and their Google Analytics so we can see how Facebook is performing and pass back Shopify data to Google Analytics. Integrate your technology platforms in Days 1-7 (Week 1) as per the 60 Day Digital Marketing Checklist.

Save yourself some time poring over data by integrating your platforms.

#3: Marketing Automation and Landing Page Templates

If you currently are not using marketing automation, then it's time to look into it. Marketing automation allows you to set up campaigns and nurture prospects using email and other touch points.

Marketing automation are email funnels that you set up with your marketing automation platforms. You drip out emails with content or promotions to your prospects to ascend them through your buying process.

The best part of marketing automation is once you set it up, it runs automatically based on how you want to nurture your prospects and on the prospects' behavior. You are saving time by not manually tending to prospects AND it also gives you time back to work on your business!

I include landing page templates with marketing automation because you use landing pages as part of your marketing automation funnels.

Landing page templates save a lot of time. With templates, you can set up a landing page within minutes. If you want a more in-depth page, the setup might take a bit longer, for example if you want to include more copy and, say, videos. But a well-designed page with graphics and sales components can be created in mere minutes to start off your sales process. I go more deeply into landing pages in Chapter 8, and more information on marketing automation can be found in Chapter 9.

There are several landing page platforms that I use, such as LeadPages, Optimizepress and Unbounce. All are good resources to get started with landing pages, and all are user-friendly. I've included links to these in the Resources at the end of this chapter.

#4: Social Media Automation

You are probably posting on social media right now. If you aren't, you should look into having a social media presence.

Social media posting can seem daunting—yet another task you have to do. But it can be very easy if you use the right tools. I generated a very simple method to post social media.

I create a social media calendar (find a sample content calendar in the Resources section at the end of the chapter). I would suggest you create this once a month for the whole month. Because when you are doing it on the fly, posting to social media can be another task you have to do. Plan out all your social media posts in advance. And put them on a Google Sheet.

I have several columns in my Google Sheet: name of post, social media platform (Facebook, LinkedIn, etc), a short blurb I want to include with the post and the date. Then I use scheduling tools to schedule my posts in advance. I use tools like Hootsuite and the scheduling tool in Facebook to schedule all my posts for the week. You can do it for the month or the week. After you've created your calendar, all you need to do is create the post, copy and paste your blurb and schedule the post. It will take you an hour to do that once a month and you have all your social media posts ready to go live.

Social media automation has saved me a lot of time.

#5: Outsourcing

This is applicable for all entrepreneurs, but especially if you are a solo-preneur. You are probably finding that running a business isn't an easy task.

Your biggest mistake is doing everything yourself. Your business can slide right under you because you are juggling too many things at once. I recommend outsourcing.

You might say that's expensive. However, there are plenty of options that allow you to outsource for as low as five dollars.

Most of you have heard about Fiverr. I have used Fiverr for a few of my projects. And I have had great experiences. Find a freelancer on Fiverr and pay them five dollars to complete a task. It's fast and easy and doesn't require a lot of explaining or descriptions up front. And it's only five dollars!

Upwork is another outsourcing platform. You can post your project and get bids. It does require going through the freelancers and reviewing their profiles. This might be useful for you for a bigger project or ongoing projects. But think about it: you might have to put some time upfront to hire a good consultant, but that consultant can save you hours in doing all those tasks yourself.

Lastly, hire a VA. You can find VAs (Virtual Assistants) on Upwork or through agencies. VAs will help you with all kinds of operational, marketing and business tasks. You can assign your tasks and have time to work on your business. VAs can be very reasonably priced, starting at five dollars per hour if you find a VA overseas. Of course, there are VAs also in the US, if you would prefer to hire someone in the US.

Find outsourcers or a Virtual Assistant during Days 1-7 (Week 1).

Your Turn

You can increase your productivity and have time to work on your business by implementing these very simple methods. If you haven't been productive or feel like you have a lot on your plate, then I highly suggest implementing these five methods to get your time back to work on your business and manage your team. Go ahead and work on implementing these 5 methods to get your productivity back on track and get time back on your side.

The next point that entrepreneurs complain to me about is the technology side of digital marketing. So let's dive deeper into the marketing technology. And how it can be a friend, not foe.

Resources

Standard Operation Procedure Document — https://goo.gl/fjWBNg
Social Media Content Calendar — https://goo.gl/cHo14p
Shopify — https://goo.gl/a1xtKP
Hootsuite — https://goo.gl/78iofJ

Landing Pages
Optimizepress — https://goo.gl/e1kGfh
Instapages — http://bit.ly/2wtrh23

Outsourcing
Fiverr — https://goo.gl/Fp8ZLr
Upwork — https://goo.gl/DEETkx

Chapter 2: I Am Not Tech Savvy

The biggest reservation about digital marketing that I see with entrepreneurs is marketing technology.

As part of growing your business, you need digital marketing. Let's face it, no matter what kind of business you are in, everyone needs some form of digital marketing because your audiences are online.

You have probably experienced this yourself. As part of growing your business, you subscribe to marketing technology platforms that are being recommended by your entrepreneur friends or small business "gurus", and then you find that you aren't using them because it's too much effort to figure this out.

Don't fret. There is a solution for this. I want to share with you the five systems that help you cut through the technology clutter— without having to feel like you need to be super coder.

Before I get into the five points, I want to mention mindset. A lot of times we have these preconceived notions that something will be difficult to figure out or will be time consuming, so we get all in our heads about it, creating worst-case scenarios, and then end up doing nothing altogether.

Yes, in the past before technology became advanced, you probably did have to be a coder to set up marketing technology systems. But now it's much easier, trust me. Let's put away our previous mindset of thinking that everything will take hours to complete and open up our minds to the possibility that this will be a piece of cake.

5 ways you don't need to be tech savvy to set up your marketing systems online

#1: WYSIWYG and Drag and Drop

Ten to fifteen years ago technology was not nearly as advanced as it is today. We are on the verge of the AI (artificial intelligence) revolution, so technology has made amazing strides over the past decade.

I have worked with hundreds of different marketing technology platforms—from email, to landing page creators, to retargeting, to marketing automation—and I would say 90% of all marketing technology platforms have WYSIWYG and drag and drop functionality.

WYSIWYG stands for "what you see is what you get." It's an old term from the HTML days, which is still relevant today. It's also referred to as Page Builder or Design Editor. Most marketing technology today is what you see is what you get. You don't need to know code to create an email newsletter anymore.

The other functionality is drag and drop. Take a piece of content in the platform, drag it, drop it and make changes to it. Done! Try it and see how easy this can be. Technology is super user friendly and very intuitive nowadays.

#2: Wizards

Wizards have become very popular with marketing technology platforms. Enter a few pieces of information, and *Viola!* you have completed your set up. If you are not familiar with a wizard, it is a user interface type that presents a user with a sequence of dialog boxes that lead the user through a series of well-defined steps. Tasks that are complex, infrequently performed, or unfamiliar may be easier to perform using a wizard (from Wikipedia).

I want to share a recent example from my own experience. A little while ago I was using GoDaddy email and my yearly contract was up. I have been thinking for about switching over to Gmail (G Suite) for some time. I felt it was much better for my business needs. I did some research and found that there is a wizard called G Suite Migration for Microsoft Outlook. At first I was a bit skeptical, so I know the feeling you must be going through when you hear me talk about technology and wizards.

I had to migrate all of my emails and calendar entries from GoDaddy to Gmail so I could have a record of all emails moving forward. I thought to myself, *what if this thing breaks down in the middle? Gives me errors. I need to migrate about 10,000 emails from all my folders.*

I am glad to say that the whole wizard process went smoothly and without a hitch. Gmail needed me to login to my GoDaddy account to update my email settings and point email to the new Gmail servers. The wizard did take a day to complete the whole process— that's because I had a lot of email—but in the end, I was extremely happy and would highly recommend G Suite Migration for Microsoft Outlook if you want to migrate from Outlook to Gmail.

This is an example of a wizard I have used with G Suite. I have also used wizards to do landing page split testing and create copy for certain type of email marketing. There are thousands of wizards out there to make your life a little easier.

#3: Marketing technology integrations between systems

These days, all major marketing technology platforms are integrated.

As I mentioned in Chapter 1, Shopify does a very good job of integrating with third party platforms through their App Store. Most of these integrations don't require you to be a coding genius. Just go into the platform, look for tabs or links marked "Integrations" and connect the platforms.

Recently I was working with the same client I mentioned in Chapter 1 to set up Welcome messages. Each welcome message was unique based on the product or products the user purchased. I was easily able to set up an Integration between MailChimp (the email platform) and Shopify (the shopping cart) to pass data back and forth to create these specific Welcome emails.

And if you haven't heard of Zapier, I would highly suggest looking into this technology. It's a way to connect many different platforms and pass back data to make a smooth technology process.

Zapier is a web automation app. With Zapier you can build Zaps which can automate parts of your business or life. A Zap is a blueprint for a task you want to do over and over. In words, a Zap looks like this: "When I get a new thing in A, do this other thing in B." The first part is the Trigger and the second part is the Action. Zapier supports hundreds of apps. You can mix and match triggers and actions to automate just about anything.

I have used Zapier in the past and was very impressed. For example, I can create a Zap when someone signs up for my email list, I can add that user to a certain segment for the user to receive more targeted marketing communications.

#4: Video how-to tutorials

You are probably saying, well that's not quick and easy. I have to watch videos.

But I assure you, video tutorials are quick and easy. They are usually around five minutes and will get you the details that you need in a snap.

The best part is that you will be able to follow along with the video as you are managing the marketing technology platform. How-to videos have been a life-saver for me many times. And these videos can be created by someone representing the platform or by a marketing technology expert. In fact, I am working on a digital marketing course now where I will have how-to videos for all the top marketing platforms. See the Next Steps chapter at the end of the book for more information.

#5: Outsourcing

As I mentioned in Chapter 1, outsourcing is useful in many ways.

If you want extra help and you don't have time or energy to figure out a marketing technology platform, I recommend outsourcing.

Again, there are plenty of options that allow you to outsource for as low as five dollars, such as Fiverr, Upwork, or to a Virtual Assistant. Check out Chapter 1 for more information about Outsourcing.

Your Turn

What these five systems mean is that you don't have to be a genius coder or development guru to use marketing technology platforms. And these platforms—along with a solid marketing strategy—are the keys to growing your business with digital marketing. If you feel like you have been drowning in marketing technology, I highly suggest making use of these systems. So take the next step and implement these 5 strategies to help you overcome your uneasiness with technology.

Now that we have tackled technology, the next big hurdle I often hear from entrepreneurs is that their business is different and they don't need digital marketing. I assure you, if you want to grow your business, then you will need some form of digital marketing.

Resources

Shopify — https://goo.gl/a1xtKP
G Suite Migration for Microsoft Outlook — https://goo.gl/KRY721
Mailchimp — https://goo.gl/kHXX4U
Zapier — https://goo.gl/zgnShN
Fiverr — https://goo.gl/Fp8ZLr
Upwork — https://goo.gl/DEETkx

Chapter 3: My Business is Different—I Don't Need Digital Marketing

I have worked with hundreds of companies at this point, from big to small, from mom and pop shops to enterprise-level corporations. And every single type of business needed digital marketing. I have yet to find a business that doesn't.

The number one reason that every business needs digital marketing is because your potential customer is online. You need a digital strategy to find, engage with and get that prospect to like and trust your business. A prospect that likes and trusts you is a lot more likely to convert to a paying customer. While the entire process may not be online, typically the process starts online.

When we talk about marketing, we think, "It's about us. It's about the business."

Wrong.

It's not about you. It's about the customer.

Marketing is not about your business being different, it's: "Where is my customer hanging out?" I can tell you that no matter what your business is, your customer is hanging out online. On Facebook. On Instagram. On Twitter. On Google. And that's how you get your customer's attention.

I can provide one example of a very niche market. I was speaking to a manufacturing association. They help manufacturing companies build and grow. We were discussing a company that manufactures components to airline companies. It's a small, niche market and the business only has a few clients because there are only a couple of dozen airline companies in the US.

The pool of prospects is small, but the manufacturer is still using digital marketing to connect with these prospects. They are using LinkedIn to create business relationships. They are also using content to educate prospects and email to disseminate the content.

Whether you are a specific niche business in the aerospace industry, or whether you have an e-commerce business, you still need to set up a system to bring in new, fresh leads.

For example, I was working with an enterprise SaaS (Software as a Service) solution and they have robust products in the $50,000-$200,000 range. Of course no one is going to whip out their credit card and put $50,000 on their Visa to buy the SaaS solution. But we set up a system to bring in new leads for the SaaS client.

- Content to engage with the prospects.
- Social media to disseminate the content and opt-ins to capture email addresses.
- Nurture funnels to engage prospects further with white papers, case studies and videos.
- Retargeting to bring prospects back to the site.

And then the sales team took over to close the deal.

Local businesses also use digital marketing to bring in new customers. Whether you are a restaurant, dentist or chiropractor, you will also need digital marketing to find new customers and engage with them over time.

When I have worked with clients who only do business locally, I set up Facebook ads and special promotions—for example, a free appetizer for a restaurant, or a special on teeth whitening for a dentist.

I also set up automated reminders for the local business so they don't have to manually remind customers to come in for the next appointment.

And of course, B2C (business to consumer) businesses that typically have a very large pool of potential customers use digital marketing heavily, from content to paid media ads, Amazon, retargeting and landing pages. Often, digital marketing is the staple strategy for consumer products.

Your Turn

Every business, big or small, local or a world conglomerate, needs some forms of digital marketing. If you have been on the fence about whether digital marketing is the right strategy for you, then I hope you found the key takeaway, which is, it's not about the *business* but it IS about the *customer*. Your customer is probably hanging out online, and in order to get his/her attention, you have to have a digital marketing strategy. So think about how you can find your ideal customer and some of the digital strategies that would work to bring them into the fold.

Now that we have ascertained that all businesses need some form of digital marketing to find the idea customer, I will dive deeper into how best to develop your customer profile.

Resources

10 reasons you need a digital marketing strategy in 2017 —
https://goo.gl/ntD2GP
10 reasons you need a digital marketing strategy —
https://goo.gl/KxvSYj
Why Small Businesses Need Online Marketing —
https://goo.gl/CejmoS

Chapter 4: Developing Your Customer Profile (Customer Avatar)

Imagine: you are sitting at your desk and going through your daily sales reports. You open up the window for your online sales reporting and see that you've made 20% more in sales than the previous week. "Wow," you think to yourself, "am I seeing that number correctly? Is it a mistake?" You dig a little deeper into the reporting and see what was sold, when it was sold and to whom. Once you realize it's all true a huge smile comes over your face and you start to do your happy dance. OK, maybe you don't do the dance, but you're ecstatic.

Now, imagine this happening to you every day, not just once in awhile or on a lucky day, but each and every day you enter your online sales reporting. You feel like you won the lottery each day by having new customers who love your product and come back for more.

I am going to share with you one of the main components I discovered that works tremendously well to bring in new prospects, the ones who are eager to buy your products or services. But, before you turn these prospects to customers, you need them to find you, and have a message that resonates with them and moves them to take action. There's a saying in the marketing world: "If you market to everyone, you sell to no one." So the first thing you need to do is get clear on your ideal target audience.

One of my private clients is in the e-learning space focusing on web development courses. The client had an amazing product and all the users of the product were giving my client raving reviews. So I knew the course was sound. By the time I engaged with my client, he was already doing well with his business, but most of his sales were coming from partnerships or referrals. My client had tried advertising on Facebook before, but complained to me that he had lackluster results with his efforts. The first thing I asked him was, did he have a customer profile developed? He looked at me like I was speaking Greek. "A what?" he said.

Many times entrepreneurs get so caught up with their product and getting it out there in the market that they forget why the product was developed in the first place. It was developed to help a certain target market and to address their challenges or solve a problem.

Most entrepreneurs think that a customer profile is just demographic data—age, sex, marital status, household income. While that's a good start, it's very broad. And in order for your marketing to be effective, you have to dig deeper.

The components of a customer profile

Components of a customer profile include:
- Goals: what do they want to accomplish?
- Where do they hang out? What are they reading? Which sites are they going to? Which celebrities or high-profile individuals do they follow?
- Pain Points: what are their challenges? Think of these as how your product/service solves their problems.
- What are some of the objections that your target market will have to your product or service?

Some other things you can ask about your target market are:
- How is their problem impacting their lives?
- Where does the customer want to be? What do the symbols of success look like?

Finding your ideal target market

When I ask my clients what their target market's pains, fears, frustrations and ambitions are the answer is usually the same —"I don't know." If that's the case for you then the first thing you need to do is very simple: ask them.

One of the best ways to gathering this information is to survey your current customers. Send out a survey via email. Call your current customers. Talk to potential customers. Use the questions above to help you identify the problems.

Another way to gather information is to research online. Use Google to find some of the components of your ideal target market. But don't be broad. For example, if your product is in the golf space, don't use Tiger Woods as a guru of the market. Although he is, that's way too broad. Find gurus who are more specific that golf aficionados would know about. Use Google to find blogs, publications, websites, books, and events that your target market would engage with.

Next, check out some social media sites. Sites such as Facebook, Instagram or LinkedIn have a great deal of insight about what customers want. If you were to ask me this ten or fifteen years ago, I would not give this is a possible answer to find your target market. Now everything is public on social media. Find your competitors' social media pages or websites, check out what their customers are saying. Review posts and comments and questions. What are their challenges and pain points? Make a note of these. It's a plethora of untapped information.

Other tools and resources

I also use Facebook Audience Insights. This is a tool within Facebook that allows you to get more insight into a certain audience. Facebook Audience Insights gives you aggregate information about audiences so you can create content that resonates and easily find more people like the ones in your current audience. You can use it to add certain interests to start off your search and Facebook will provide you closely related pages and other demographics to help you gain even further insights. For example, if I want to learn more about the running market, I would go to Facebook Audience Insights and start off with "Hal Higdon" (a well-known running coach) and then Audience Insights would also provide information about users who like Hal Higdon. It's a method to find similar audiences to your audience on Facebook.

You may also check out tools like TowerData where you can upload your current customer email list and find demographic data about your customers. According to TowerData, the tool reveals the real-time interests and wants of customers and prospects, and helps marketers reach consumers with messages about the right products at the right time—when they are actively shopping for them. You can find a link to Towerdata in the Resources section at the end of this chapter to learn more about the capabilities.

For my e-learning client who didn't know anything about the customer avatar, we went back and had him do some research and answer the customer profile questions to get a very good understanding of his target market. He sent out a survey to his email list. We also spoke to about thirty of his current clients on the phone to get more feedback. Once we implemented his target market profile in his marketing communications, he sales doubled within ninety days.

Your Turn

Get precise with your audiences. We always think broader is better, but your message gets diluted in a broad market. If you are precise and have a message that resonates with your ideal client, then your audiences will see that you understand their pain points and find your content and marketing message valuable. Customers want products and services designed specifically for them, so they can relate to the problem and get the precise solution they need.

I have included a Customer Avatar Worksheet in the Resources section below for you to review and fill out.

Reference the 60 Day Digital Marketing Checklist for Days 8-14 (Week 2) to research your customer avatar, fill out the Customer Avatar Worksheet and find data on Facebook Audience Insights.

With your new customer avatar in hand, you can now start to formulate your products. If you are reading this book, you might already have a product or service, but in the next chapter I go further of how to structure your product offerings.

Resources

Customer Avatar Worksheet — https://goo.gl/DZigei
Facebook Audience Insights — https://goo.gl/hNcYLv
TowerData — https://goo.gl/8znbde

Chapter 5: Product Offering Strategy

You have created a product or multiple products in your business. And now you want to get your products out to the ideal target market. That's the plan, but first we need to create a product offering strategy to formulate your products.

A product strategy is a method to organize your products which allows you to build your brand, nurture your customers and bring in revenue for your business.

When I first engage with a client, the client usually has just one product. For example, a coaching program or an online course. Typically these products or services have higher price points. This is when I come in as the digital marketing expert to build out a product offering strategy for a client.

Here I would recommend my client add in multiple smaller products to build up to your main offer—what we call the Core Offer—the coaching services or the online course, for example.

Why you need a product offering strategy

If you offer only a high price-point product to a brand-new prospect, that might scare them off. It's a lot of money. It's a big commitment. Instead of presenting these prospects with your high price-point core offer right away, we start off with bite-size pieces. We offer your prospects some content, and if they engage, then we offer them a smaller price-point product—say ten dollars or twenty dollars—and so on and so forth.

This allows the prospect to get to know your mission, your company and your brand. Over time they get to know, trust and like you. And at the end, when you offer your prospect your higher price-point core offer, it's a natural progression of their engagement with your brand. At that point, they are ready to take the next step and buy your product or service.

The product strategy is typically incorporated into your content strategy and nurture funnels to communicate the benefits of these products to your prospects. I go into content strategy in Chapter 6 and nurture funnels in Chapter 9.

What a product offering strategy looks like

A product strategy is designed around nurturing and engaging with your prospects. Again, we don't want to start off with a scary, high price-point offer. We want to weave that into a bigger strategy that starts off with bite-size pieces, and then we ascend the prospect to the next level each time.

#1: Content

Typically marketers don't think of this is a product, but I incorporate content into the product offering strategy. It's a very important piece of driving awareness to prospects who have never heard of your brand. Content should be engaging. It should tell a story and it should leave your prospect wanting more at the end. It can be in the form of a video, blog post, article or another easily consumable format. I go more into content in Chapter 6.

#2: Lead Magnet to capture opt-in

Once the prospect has engaged with your content, continue to engage with them with a free, more in-depth product. In the digital marketing industry, it's called a Lead Magnet. Lead Magnets are typically a free piece of content that draws the user in where the business can ask them for their email address and plug that into a lead capture. Lead magnets can be anything from a report, checklist, e-book, white paper or a PDF: basically a piece of content that allows the user to learn more about your products, brand and expertise. The idea is to engage with the prospect even more and provide more in-depth content and also capture the prospect's contact information via an opt-in form.

#3: Low price-point product to gain a win or a micro commitment

If the prospect has engaged with your Lead Magnet, take them to the next level. Offer them a low price-point product—say ten to twenty dollars. A lot of times I get the response: "I don't have such a product offering." If you don't have such a product, then you can create one. For example, for one of my clients who has an e-learning program, we took one of the twelve modules and made that into a low price-point product of ten dollars. We gave the user a small taste of the whole e-learning course, but it was for only ten dollars. And if the user bought the ten-dollar module, we gave them a ten-dollar discount for the full e-learning course, since they already paid that amount.

If you have a service business, you can try offering a free or low cost thirty-minute consultation.

For SaaS (Software as a Service) products, offer a free short-term trial.

#4: Core offer

This is the product offering that most businesses already have created. This can be your SaaS (Software as a Service) product, consulting services, your e-learning course or a physical product. Again, if your prospect has engaged with your small price-point product, then offer them this core offer as the logical next step.

#5: Upsells

After your customer purchased the core offer, there are additional offerings you can provide. They are called upsells and these can be other complimentary products in your business. For example, if you have an e-learning product about how to run a cake decorating business, you might want to offer "Email Listing Building Strategy for Your Cake Decorating Business" e-learning product as an upsell. These are stand-along products that are related to your core offer.

#6: Downsells

Typically downsells are product offerings for users who have not purchased your core offer. A downsell strategy would be to provide a payment plan for your core offer. For example, if you core offer is one thousand dollars, then offer your prospect a downsell of four monthly payments of two hundred and fifty dollars each.

The biggest mistake entrepreneurs make when it comes to product offers

The biggest mistake I see is that a business has only ONE product to offer their prospects. This becomes an issue because the entire marketing budget is used to promote this one product. Acquiring new customers does require a certain budget. And sometimes it might cost more to acquire a new customer than the value of the ONE product. To avoid this issue, create more product offerings for your customers. Upsell current customers through email or retargeting methods, which are very low cost. Any upsells will be additional revenue for your business. For example, let's say it costs you ten dollars to acquire a new customer. You just acquired a new customer, let's call her Sally. Sally just spend five dollars with you. So you had to spend ten dollars to acquire Sally as a new customer, but Sally only spend five dollars. So right now, you are upside down on your customer acquisition strategy. To recoup the other five dollars to break even on your customer acquisition, offer Sally upsells. Let's say Sally then buys a twenty dollar product and a fifty dollar product. In the end, Sally has spent seventy-five dollars with you and it took you ten dollars to acquire Sally as a customer. So you just made sixty five dollars!

Your Turn

A product offering strategy will allow you to engage with your prospects. And an engaged prospect is a lot more likely to purchase your product or services.

If you haven't been seeing the results you desire for your business and you want to get customers who are coming in on auto-pilot and eventually purchasing your products, then take the 6 steps I mentioned in this chapter (Content, Lead Magnet, low priced offer, Core Offer, Upsells and Downsells) and use them to create your own product flow to entice users to engage with you. Use the 60 Day Digital Marketing Checklist (Days 15-21 - Week 3) to create your product offering strategy and your products.

We are getting a solid foundation for your digital marketing. Now that we have your ideal target market and your product offerings, we can start creating content.

Chapter 6: Content Strategy

A content strategy is way to interact with your prospects and even your customers to communicate valuable information to them. A content strategy also ties in closely to your product offering strategy.

I am going to introduce a new funnel concept here – top of the funnel, middle of the funnel and bottom of the funnel. I will go more in depth into the three stages of the funnel in Chapter 9, Nurture Funnels/Marketing Automation, but it is important to understand the funnel for content.

The top of the funnel you are building awareness with your prospects. These are users who have never heard of you. These prospects are getting to know you and learning about your mission, products and services.

The middle of the funnel are users who have interacted with your brand but have not purchased yet. These users know a little about your brand, probably have been to your site or your social media pages and have already interacted with some of your content. This is where you bring in more valuable content and engage with your prospects even further.

The bottom of the funnel is the conversion. At this point the prospect is whipping out their credit card to purchase your product or calling up your sales person to finish closing the deal.

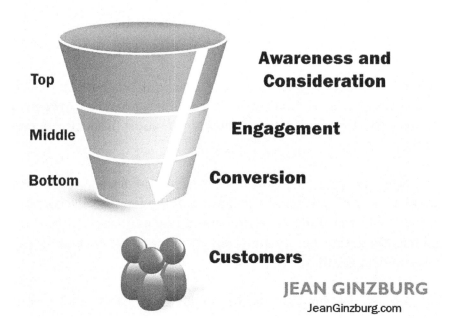

You want to drive awareness at the top of the funnel with engaging content to bring users in and, then move the users down the funnel to the middle by incorporating more in-depth content. At the bottom of the funnel, you close.

Examples of content

At the top of the funnel you use videos, blog posts, articles, and/or checklists. These pieces of content are typically specific, short and engaging. An example could be a checklist to set up your Facebook campaign, or a video on how to prepare for your first marathon.

At the middle of the funnel, the prospect is already engaged and would like to learn more about your mission or products/services. This content is typically longer and can include in-depth videos and blog posts, reports, case studies and white papers.

Components of a successful content strategy

The components of a content strategy include the following:
- Survey your audiences.
- Understand their pain points and challenges.
- Create content to address these challenges.
- Create a content calendar.
- Distribute content.

Let's dive into these in more detail.

#1: Create a survey to better understand what your customers need or want

We covered this also in Chapter 4, Developing Your Customer Profile. At this stage, you would want to create questions to get deeper into the pain points and challenges of your customers. This survey can be in the form of an email or phone calls. And don't worry, if you are just getting started and don't have customers, then survey your prospects or individuals who might be interested in your products/services.

#2: Gather pain points and challenges from your survey

As you get to know your prospects and customers more over time, you'll see that there is a common list of about ten questions/pain points/frustrations or so—it might be more if you are selling a complex product such as a SaaS (Software as a Service) solution or service.

#3: Address pain points and challenges

One of the main questions I get from clients and prospects is, "What should my content be about?"

You've already surveyed your customers. You have filled out your Customer Avatar Worksheet from Chapter 4. You have gathered the pain points and frustrations. Now create content to address these pain points and challenges, and to answer common questions.

At the top of the funnel, where you are driving awareness for brand new prospects who haven't heard from you, content answers common, introductory questions your users have. These answers can be in the form of a blog post, article or video.

For example, if you are in the running space, and a prospect wants to start a running program, they might have questions such as, "How do I get started with a running program?" or "What kinds of shoes do I need to buy?"

At this point, your new potential customer can further engage with your brand to better grasp if your product/service is right decision for them.

At the middle of the funnel, the prospect has already learned about your business and your expertise. You have identified your authority on the subject and the prospect is ready to engage further.

At the middle of the funnel is where you target the prospect with more in-depth content. This content will further answer the user's questions and gets him/her deeper into the topic. This is where you would want to present them with a Lead Magnet (see Chapter 5, #2 – Product Offering Strategy) It can be in the form of a report, article, checklist, white paper, or video with more in-depth content.

With a Lead Magnet, the user will opt-in to your content and with their contact information and then you can provide them with additional content so they can learn more about your brand, mission and products/services. Continue to send valuable content to your prospects to ascend them in the funnel. Additionally, customers also want to hear from you and receive engaging content, so it's not just prospects.

#4: Create a content calendar

Once you have created content, the next step is to distribute it across your social media channels.

It's crucial that you stay organized with your content. A content calendar has saved me a ton of time in my business, as I shared in Chapter 1. I have a Google Sheet that I share with my team. I plan all my content and social media posts in advance and then use a social media planning tool such as Hootsuite to schedule all the posts in advance. It will save you a lot of time. I shared the link to my Content Calendar in Google Sheets in the Resources Section at the end of this chapter.

#5: Distribute content

Once you have created your content calendar, then distribute your content using social media automation. I went into details of how to automate your social media in Chapter 1, Point #4.

Use social media such as Facebook, LinkedIn, Twitter or other social media platforms you use in your business to distribute content. This allows your prospects to engage with you and your brand on your social media channels. You can also use advertising on Facebook to distribute this content to new audiences. I go further on Facebook advertising in Chapter 7. Additionally, I have also used content distribution networks such as or Taboola, Outbrain and Content.ad.

That's how you create a content strategy. The best part is you can automate this by scheduling all your content posts in advance, nurturing your users with in-depth content and eventually converting your prospects to paying customers.

Your Turn

Once you create a content strategy for your business, you can engage prospects and allow them to get to know your brand and your company. Engaged users are the ones that purchase products or services.

Now it's your turn to use your Customer Avatar Worksheet that you created in Chapter 4, address your customers' pain points and create content around those frustrations. Then create a content calendar and distribute your content across your social media channels, email and content distribution networks.

Now that you are on Days 22-28 (Week 4), review your 60 Day Digital Marketing Checklist and complete the steps.

After you have created your content and received some feedback from your audiences organically, then the next step is to run Facebook ads to your content.

Resources

Social Media Content Calendar — https://goo.gl/cHo14p
Hootsuite — https://goo.gl/78iofJ
Taboola — https://goo.gl/ofKVR1
Outbrain — https://goo.gl/PW2fcK
Content.ad — https://goo.gl/LNnxN1

Chapter 7: Facebook Advertising

If you use Facebook, you probably have seen ads in your news feed. Facebook advertising has been around since 2012 and it has been the most successful marketing platform for advertisers in the past few years.

Why is it so successful? Because at the time of the publication of this book, there are two billion users on Facebook. Facebook and Google combined will account for 89 percent of digital ad spend growth in 2017. Also in 2017, digital ad spend is predicted to surpass TV ad spend for the first time. These are very strong data points, which is why Facebook advertising has been a staple for businesses for years now.

Also, Facebook metrics are still very reasonable. Most online advertising pricing models are auctions and use Cost per Click (CPC) – the amount a click costs – and Cost per 1000 Impressions (CPM) – the amount that 1000 impressions cost. For Facebook, the CPC and CPMS are still at an affordable rate for small businesses. If you haven't started running Facebook ads, then there is no time like the present.

I use Facebook ads to drive fresh leads into the funnel (more on that in Chapter 10). The reason is that Facebook has very granular targeting which allows you to find any target market. I have not found any other paid media platform to be as granular.

To get you started setting up your first Facebook campaign, I am going to cover the 5 Components of a Successful Facebook Campaign. But before we get started, you first need to install your Facebook pixel on your site. I created the Facebook Pixel Guide for Wordpress, Shopify and SquareSpace which walks you thought how to install your Facebook pixel on these platforms (see Resources section at the end of this chapter.)

5 components of a successful Facebook campaign

The five components of a successful ad campaign on Facebook are as follows:

- Targeting
- Headlines
- Copy
- Your visual ad unit
- Your call to action

#1: Targeting

One of the main appeals of Facebook advertising versus other digital marketing platforms is the targeting capabilities. Facebook has extremely granular targeting based on users' demographic data, interests and purchase data. And targeting is extremely crucial when it comes to Facebook ads. If you are not targeting the right audiences, whether you have an awesome video, a solid headline, or amazing copy, you are not going to get the results that you're looking for.

You can target users by demographics, for example sex, age and geolocation. Facebook also uses third party data for purchase behavior—for example credit card data. Facebook can tell if a user is in the market for a particular product based on user behavior.

The third component of targeting is interests and page likes. You can target users who like certain pages and I find this to be the most effective way of targeting.

Targeting is extremely important. You have to hone in on this in order to get your audiences right. If you have not done so, please go back to Chapter 4 to create your ideal target market.

#2: Headlines

Create a snappy headline so users notice your ad as they are scrolling through their feed. You want to make sure that you are getting their attention. Of course you do not want to be deceiving, but you want to make sure that you're getting a pattern interrupt when you create your ad. This makes headlines an important piece of the ad, because the headline is the first thing users see in addition to, of course, your visual component. For inspiration on headlines, take a look at magazines or high-converting landing pages. For headlines, it's best to create a sense of urgency or have an air of mystery to grab the user's attention.

#3: Ad copy

Copy is also extremely important. What I have seen working lately has been more colloquial ad copy, for example, "Hi. I'm Jean Ginzburg and I'm the CEO of Ginball Digital Marketing and today I want to talk about how to set up a Facebook campaign." You're talking to your audiences versus writing marketing copy. Be more open, more authentic.

#4: Visual ad

Your visual component can be an image or a video. Lately, video has been working well for acquiring new customers and driving acquisition and awareness. As an example, I was working on a campaign for one of my current clients and we were running side-by-side an image and a video ad on Facebook. The video ad was outperforming the image. It was costing us about a dollar to acquire a new customer with video and two dollars to acquire a new customer with the image ad. Be sure to incorporate video ads into your Facebook ad strategy.

As for the messaging, tell a compelling story in your video. Provide value to your audiences. Share content that your audiences would be interested in. Also, be sure to add captions to the bottom of your video. This tremendously increases engagement.

#5: Call to action

You want to make sure that you're matching your call to action with your campaign. Is it a "Download Now" button, is it a "Buy Now" button, or is it a "Learn More"? The call to action must match what you are offering in your ad so consumers are not confused.

As you are setting up your Facebook ad, you will also need to include a landing page. That's where you will be driving your traffic. I go further into landing pages in the next chapter (Chapter 8).

Analytics

Below are main analytics metrics you should be reviewing when you launch your Facebook ads campaigns.

- Reach – the number of people who saw your ad at least once. If your reach is low (below 2000 impressions) then the rest of your analytics will also be low. To gain more reach, increase your audience and your budget
- Results – the number of times your ad achieved an outcome based on the objective you selected. This would translate into the number of completed registrations or website purchases. Keep an eye on this metric as it will let you know your number of conversions.
- Frequency – the average number of times each person saw your ad. This figure should be no more than 5. If you are getting above 10, then your frequency is very high. At this point, either increase your audiences or increase your budget.
- Cost Per Result – the average cost per result. When you set up your Facebook ads, Facebook will optimize for certain results, for example, for completed registrations, or clicks or website purchases. With respect to the cost per results, if you are running a lead campaign, then your cost per results should be $2-10 for consumer products and $20-100 for business products. Again, these are just benchmarks. You

should also check your internal analytics to better understand how much you can pay to acquire a new customer.

- Engagement (reactions, shares, comments) – how many users are reacting (liking, loving, etc), sharing or commenting on your ad. If you are not seeing any engagement with your ads, it means that either your audiences are not interested in your ad or product or your messaging is off. Fix those items to continue running ads.
- Cost Per Click – the average cost for each click. Typically CPCs on Facebook are around $0.50 - $5 (the time of publication of this book). If your CPCs are much higher, then your ads might not be very relevant to your audiences. Retool your audiences.
- Budget – the daily spend for your ad set. This stat is set on the ad set level (not the campaign level). Start off with $10 per day per ad set. Once you see favorable results, then increase your budget by 50% every 3-5 days. If you increase your budget quickly – say you go from $10 per day to $100 per day – your costs per acquisition (CPA) will very likely increase. To keep CPAs to a favorable level, increase your budget gradually.
- Click through rate – the percentage of times people saw your ad and performed a click. The metric is clicks divided by impressions. The average click through rate for Facebook ads is about 1-2%. If your metrics are lower then improve your ad design or audience, because the ad might not be relevant for your audiences.
- Relevance Score – a rating from 1 to 10 that estimates how well your target audience is responding to your ad. Rule of thumb is 7-10. If you getting a low Relevance Score, refine your audiences. See Chapter 4 – Creating Your Customer Profile.
- Website Purchases – the number of pixel events tracked by your pixel. This will vary based on your products/services, but keep in mind how many website purchases you are

receiving vs. how much you are spending. If you are spending more than the total revenue you are receiving for running these ads, then you would want to create Upsells for your users to purchase to make up the loss on the Facebook ads investment (see Chapter 5 – Product Offering Strategy).

Your Turn

Facebook ads will allow you to engage with your prospects. Facebook advertising is a granular, targeted way to drive awareness for your brand, and for users to engage and learn more about your business. An engaged prospect is a lot more likely to purchase your products or services.

Now that you have learned about the 5 Components of a Successful Facebook campaign, login to your Facebook Ads Manager and create your first Facebook campaign using the strategies I discussed in this chapter.

Implement your Facebook ads creation during Days 29-35 (Week 5). Take a look at the 60 Day Digital Marketing Checklist to review the steps.

With your Facebook campaign set up, the next step is to create landing pages to send traffic from your Facebook ads. In the next chapter, I am going to go over landing pages and how best to create them.

Resources

Facebook Pixel Guide for Wordpress, Shopify and SquareSpace — https://jeanginzburg.com/fbpixel

Chapter 8: Landing Pages

Landing pages are an extremely important piece of your marketing strategy. This is where your customers interact with your brand and your product and make a purchase.

Your users see your advertisement or a piece of content and land on your page to interact with you. They learn more about your company and your products. This is also the place where they make a decision to buy or not to buy. Needless to say, it is a significant part of your marketing strategy.

The #1 mistake businesses make when it comes to landing pages

The biggest mistake is that businesses don't use landing pages.

A lot of times I might click on a link or click on an offer and it will take me to a brand's home page versus getting me to a landing page which is a lot better at converting. These businesses are losing many conversions because they're sending users to a home page. A home page is designed for informational items about your company; it's not designed to convert users to buy your products or to sign up for opt-in forms or a lead generation campaign.

Where to use landing pages

I've seen good results with using landing pages in direct response channels, such as Google Adwords, Facebook, and email marketing. Direct response channels are designed to create an immediate response and compel prospects to take some specific action such as opt-in to a free product or purchase a product. To increase conversions, you want to send that traffic to a landing page so that your user can convert.

Landing pages are used for all types of offers, including Lead Magnets (see Chapter 5 where I clarify Lead Magnets), sales pages, webinar sign-up pages, newsletter sign-up pages and free trials.

Architecture of a landing page

Here are the 5 Components of an Optimized Landing pages:
1. Headline
2. Main copy
3. Hidden navigation
4. Social sharing options
5. Call to action

#1 Headline

I discussed creating headlines in Chapter 7 - Facebook Advertising. Create an interesting, eye-catching headline that will entice your prospect to take further action.

#2 Main Copy

Then you want to have some copy, preferably in bullet points, that describes what your offer is and why they should sign up, such as the benefits they will receive. For opt-in pages or webinar sign-up pages, keep your copy short and to the point. For sales pages, you will want to write longer copy explaining the benefits of the product. If applicable, include a video in your landing page to complement the copy.

#3 Hidden Navigation

It's pertinent to keep your navigation hidden on a landing page. The navigation is the menu with links you see on top of a website. You don't want to have any links at the top of your landing page back to your home page or any other pages on your website. You want your users to be focused on the offer on the landing page.

#4 Social Sharing

Social sharing buttons are also important so that the user can share on their Facebook or Twitter or LinkedIn. It helps with getting your offer distributed across social media networks.

#5 Call to Action

For a landing page Call to Action, create a button at the bottom that takes prospects to the next step, whether it's a lead capture or a product purchase page. Make sure the button is prominent on the page and easy for prospects to see. The last thing you would want an interested prospect to do is not know how to take the next step in the process.

When you are creating landing pages, refer back to the Products Offering Chapter (Chapter 5). You will need to create landing pages for your content, Lead Magnet, low-priced point prdouct, Core Offer and any Upsells and Downsells. So use the 5 points above to create your landing pages for all products.

Once you are ready to create your landing page, I would recommend using a landing page software to make sure that you're converting your users when they land on your pages. Landing page software is designed to increase your conversions. Creating a landing page on your own can be require coding and tends to be time consuming. Landing page software make this whole process a lot easier. Here are some of the main features of landing page platforms/software:

- Customizable templates
- Mobile-responsive pages
- Confirmation (thank you) pages
- Widgets: countdown timers, social media sharing buttons, video embed, testimonial boxes and many more
- Form builders (for your Lead Magnet opt-in)

- Integrations with other platforms such as email marketing platforms, Facebook, Instagram, Google Analytics, etc.
- Analytics: heatmaps, pixel tracking and reports

All of these landing page platforms integrate easily with your website to become a high-converting tool to engage with your prospects and customers. The pricing ranges from $20-60 per month for subscription-based landing page platforms. For one-time fee platforms, those are typically around $100 one-time fee. I included a few landing page platforms I have used in the Resources section at the end of this chapter.

Analytics

Below are critical analytics to review when you are running campaigns with landing pages.
- Visitor Duration – the amount of time a visitor has stayed on your page. If your visitor duration is only a few seconds on average, then again, you would want to create more engaging content to keep visitors on your page longer.
- Form Abandonment Rate – the percentage of users who are abandoning your form. If your form abandonment is very high, say over 50%, then here are a few items you can improve on. Make your form more visually appealing. Don't require shoppers to register for an account before buying.
- Conversion Rate – the percentage of users converting on your page. There are a few possible conversion rates. The typical ones are completing a registration and making a purchase. For completing a registration, a good conversion rate to strive for is 50%. For website purchases, the average conversion rate is 3-20% depending on the flow of the consumer experience. If the consumer goes directly from an ad to a landing page, then the conversion rate is closer to 3%. If the consumer has been nurtured over a period of time and then presented with a purchase, then the conversion rate is closer to 20%.

Your Turn

Landing pages are a key piece of you digital marketing strategy. This is where prospects get their first impression of your brand and company. Use the 5 points in this chapter to create your landing pages.

In Days 36-42 (Week 6) you will be creating your landing pages. Refer back to the 60 Day Digital Marketing Checklist to mark off the steps.

Now that you have created your Facebook campaign and the landing page where you will be sending your Facebook traffic, you want your prospect to further interact with your brand. So to continue to nurture that prospect relationships, the next step is to set up a nurture funnel.

Resources

Clickfunnels — https://goo.gl/fC44yc
Optimizepress — https://goo.gl/e1kGfh
LeadPages — https://goo.gl/928pa9
Unbounce — https://goo.gl/CpW57i
Instapages — http://bit.ly/2wtrh23

JEAN GINZBURG

Chapter 9: Nurture Funnels/Marketing Automation

About 3 percent of users purchase a product on the first try. This number was larger about 15 years ago when the internet was in its infancy. But these days it's much harder to convert a potential customer on the first try. It takes multiple touch points for the user to become aware of your brand/products, learn more about your mission, and eventually convert to a paying customer.

A couple of years ago I started working with a client in the health/fitness space. They had a paleo product and at the time we started our engagement, the client didn't have a sales funnel. He was driving ad traffic to a landing page and getting about a 3% conversion. This means he was missing about 97% of the potential customers. That's a lot!

He was following up with his prospects, but it was sporadic and there was no process in place. Potential sales were slipping through the cracks. My client said, "I just don't have the time to follow up with all these prospects." This a common challenge I see in businesses but there is a solution.

The solution is creating a nurture funnel.

Benefits of a nurture funnel

There are a few benefits of a nurture funnel:
- It allows you to nurture your prospects over time.
- These prospects get to know, like and trust you.
- And at the end of the funnel when you ask them for the sale, they are eager to buy your products or services.

We have covered the top, middle and bottom of the funnel in Chapters 5 and 6 as the funnel was relevant to product strategy and content strategy. We will also be covering the top, middle and bottom of the funnel in this chapter as it relates to nurturing your prospects. As I mentioned in my introduction, everything in digital marketing is interrelated. And concepts can be applied to several strategies in your digital marketing framework.

The top of the funnel you are building awareness with your prospect. These prospects are getting to know you and learning about your mission, products and services. This begins with the prospect searching for something. Perhaps the prospect has a problem or a need and he or she is looking for a specific product or service. For example, the prospect is interested in starting a running program.

So the prospect starts doing some searches on Google or Facebook or Instagram. This is where you come in with your funnel. You provide the prospect with content at the top of the funnel. Content is typically answers to common questions that your users have. These answers can be in the form of a blog post, article or video. At this stage, the prospect has the opportunity to engage with you, learn more about your business and better understand if your product or service is the right next step.

The middle of the funnel are users who have interacted with your brand but have not purchased yet. At this point the prospect has already learned about your business and your expertise. You have identified your authority on the subject and the prospect is ready to engage further.

This is where you target the prospect with a Lead Magnet (See Chapter 5, #2 – Product Offering Strategy). This product will further answer the user's questions and gets him/her deeper into the topic and can be in the form of a report, article, checklist, white paper, or video with more in-depth content. In exchange for this Lead Magnet, the prospect will give you his or her contact information.

With their contact information, you can continue to nurture your prospect. The middle of the funnel will vary in terms of length. The prospect might need more nurture with white papers and reports to make a decision. It depends on your product. If the product or service is relatively easy to internalize and has a lower price point, then the middle of the funnel is shorter. If you are selling a much more complex product, for example an enterprise SaaS (Software as a Service) solution, then the middle of the funnel can take weeks or months.

The bottom of the funnel is the smallest part of the funnel, but the most concentrated. By then, the users are familiar with your company, they have engaged with you and expressed an interest and are ready to buy. The prospect might have some final questions. At this point it's best to schedule a consultation or have your sales support answer any questions. Or if your product is an e-commerce product, this typically doesn't require any additional questions. The prospect will purchase your product through your email sequence or through an ad.

You have converted your prospect into a customer. All of this is set up through a marketing automation platform which allows you to create your campaigns ahead of time and nurture prospects over time without having to do anything manually.

We should think of these nurture campaigns as relationships. We are still interacting with people, which means that we should nurture people through these funnels as we are nurturing any relationship.

Let me give you a real-world example. I am sitting at a coffee shop, doing work and I see an interesting person sitting at another table. I approach that person and ask her, "Would you be my best friend?" Well that's just weird and awkward...

Or I am at a bar and I see an attractive man and I come up to him and say, "Will you marry me?" Again, inappropriate...

As with any relationship—it takes time. We start off by engaging with that person via email or text message, then asking them out for coffee, then learning more about them, then going to dinner and so on and so forth.

The biggest mistake businesses make: they don't nurture

The biggest mistakes I see with businesses who are trying to sell a product or service is that they push the sale WAY too quickly. Things take time. Engagement takes time. That's why it's called a nurture funnel.

Circling back to my health and fitness client who was struggling to respond to his prospects, we worked on creating a funnel for this client's coaching service. We used a variety of touch points: blog posts, videos, emails and retargeting ads to engage and bring users into the funnel.

Once we were done setting everything up and pushed the "on" button and prospects started funneling in, the client doubled his revenue within a month. And that was just in the first month! It grew even more as the months went by.

We created a nurture funnel that was running on auto-pilot. The client was making money while he was sleeping because we set everything up to be automated. AND the client also freed up his day so he wasn't manually nurturing prospects and he was able to use this time to manage his team and work on developing more products.

Most nurture funnels or marketing automation funnels are set up using marketing automation platforms. They typically have similar functions and have the following capabilities:

- Marketing sequences
- Moving users from one sequence to another based on behavior
- Tagging contacts
- Email broadcasts

Most marketing automation platforms range between $10-75 per months depending on capabilities. I have included several marketing automation platforms in the Resources section at the end of this chapter. Most of the platforms (except for Infusionsoft) are all similar with respect to features. They all integrate with your shopping cart (Shopify, WooCommerce, etc) and other marketing platforms to create a smooth technology stack. Infusionsoft starts at $250 per month because it also acts as a shopping cart, CRM (customer relationship manager) and digital product delivery system. And only certain businesses will need such a robust platform as Infusionsoft. Otherwise I would stick with one of the other 5 platforms.

Your Turn

Now that you have learned about nurture funnels, then the next step is to create one of your own. Sign up for a marketing automation platform (see Resources section) and create messages to bring your prospects in to the funnel and ascend them so they can get to know you and your brand better. And when you ask them for the sale at the bottom of the funnel, they are ready to buy!

Over the next two weeks – Days 43-56 (Weeks 7 and 8) you will be creating your nurture funnels. Since nurture funnels are more time consuming than other campaigns – it requires copywriting and platform set-up, I have allotted 2 weeks for this process. Review the 60 Day Digital Marketing Checklist to check off the steps for nurture funnels.

You have accomplished a great deal so far with this book if you have been following the steps in each chapter. You are almost done! The hard part is over. The final step in the process is to create a retargeting campaign to bring back users who have previously engaged with your brand.

Analytics

Below are important email marketing analytics to review when running marketing automation/email campaigns.

- Open rate – the percentage of users who opened your email. The average email open rate is 20%. If you are getting a much lower rate, then test out different subject lines to make the message more enticing to your user.
- Click rate – the percentage of users who clicked on a link in your email. The average click through rate is 2-5%. If you are seeing lower rates for your emails, test out different email copy to engage your user.

- Unsubscribe rate – the percentage of users who unsubscribed from your email campaign. The average unsubscribe rate is about 1%.
- Abuse rate – the percentage of users who labeled your email message as spam. You want to keep this metric as low as possible. Most email marketing providers will send you a warning if your abuse rate gets too high, typically above 0.05%, but it varies by email marketing platform.

Resources

Drip Marketing — http://bit.ly/2juHhzx
Active Campaign — https://goo.gl/9M2DW7
Aweber — https://goo.gl/CuipPF
Get Response — https://goo.gl/WABa1R
Mailchimp — https://goo.gl/kHXX4U
Infusionsoft — http://bit.ly/2yahQ9F

Chapter 10: Retargeting

We are on our last step of the framework – retargeting!

Retargeting is a process to bring users and traffic back to your site or to your Facebook page: re-connecting with warm audiences who have already visited your site. Those audiences already know a little bit about you, but they haven't taken an action with you. They haven't opted-in or made a purchase. The tremendous thing about Retargeting is that once it's setup, it works on auto-pilot for the most part.

Retargeting is important because the more a prospect knows about your business and your brand, the more likely they are to take action and purchase. Retargeting focuses on a pool of users who are already familiar with your brand. This allows you access to users who are more likely to buy.

One of the main benefits of retargeting is the very efficient pricing. These campaigns have low spend and very high results and conversion because these users are more likely to purchase. You can run five dollars per day in retargeting traffic and get major results.

The easiest way to set up retargeting would be to create a campaign in Facebook. You can use other platforms such as Google Display Network, Adroll and Retargeter, which I will discuss later in this chapter.

The messaging for your remarketing ads is considered to be for "warm traffic". Warm traffic means the prospect is already aware of your brand and maybe even your products or services, but the prospect has only engaged with your brand, not taken an action. You would want to soften the message. For example, say, "Looks like you didn't purchase, or you didn't opt into that lead magnet, maybe time got in the way or things got in the way or work got in the way, so here's another chance for you to do that." That's simple messaging. Make it less sales-y.

How to set up retargeting

Facebook retargeting is for users who engage with your brand on Facebook. To set up retargeting on Facebook, there four methods:
1. Retargeting your website visitors on Facebook
2. Retarget your email list on Facebook
3. Retarget user who have engaged with your videos
4. Retarget user who have engaged with your Facebook page

Before we get into these, you first need to set up your Facebook pixel. I created the Facebook Pixel Guide for WordPress, SquareSpace and Shopify to help you do this (see Resources section at the end of this chapter). If you are using any of these platforms, check out the guide.

#1: Retargeting your website visitors on Facebook

Once you have set up your Facebook pixel, you can then set up an audience in your Facebook Ads manager. Go to the Settings bars on the upper left-hand corner and select
- Audiences
- Create Audience
- Custom Audience
- Website Traffic

Here you can select to create audiences for your entire site—for example, anyone who has visited your site. Or you can select certain pages. For example, if you have an opt-in page, you can retarget users who have landed on your opt-in page, but did not complete the registration.

You can also exclude users who have opted-in, and who visited the confirmation page. That way you aren't messaging users who have already taken an action. You have probably experienced this when you get retargeting ads for something you just purchased. That can be a little bothersome; you just purchased that product and wonder why they are retargeting you. I would suggest excluding any users who have already opted-in or purchased.

#2: Retargeting your email list on Facebook

If you are experiencing that a certain percentage of your email list are not opening up your emails, one of the ways I have found to re-engage users on an email list is to retarget them in Facebook.

You can upload your entire list of users from your email list to Facebook. Facebook will match the user by first name, last name and email address. The email address has to be a registered email address on the Facebook platform, otherwise Facebook will not recognize it. One thing to keep in mind is the match rate. If you use email addresses only, your match rate from the list to Facebook users is typically 50 percent. If you have the first and last name and email address, then the match rate can be up to 80 percent.

To set up your email list for retargeting in Facebook, download your entire list into a CSV file.

Go to the Setting bars on the upper left-hand corner in Facebook. Then and select
- Audiences
- Create Audience
- Custom Audience
- Customer File

Follow the prompts to upload your email list.

#3: Video retargeting in Facebook

You can now retarget audiences who have engaged with your videos. This is a powerful addition to Facebook retargeting. If a user has engaged with your video, this is a huge indicator they are interested in your brand or your products. With Facebook video retargeting, you can create audiences who have watched 25 percent, 50 percent or 95 percent of your video. If someone has watched 95 percent of your video, that's solid engagement!

To set up video engagement audiences, go to your Facebook Ad Manager. Once you are in Ads Manager, go to the Setting bars on the upper left-hand corner and select
- Audiences
- Create Audience
- Custom Audience
- Engagement
- Video

Choose your engagement: 25 percent, 50 percent or 95 percent of engagement with your video. Then select the videos that your users have engaged with. Follow the prompts and create your audience.

After you have set up your audiences using the three methods above, set up your Facebook ads. Again, create messaging that's softer and not sales-y. When you create your Facebook ad, make sure to choose the audience that you set up through retargeting website visitors, your email list or video engagement.

#4: Retargeting users who have engaged with your Facebook Page
Additionally, you can retarget users who have engaged with your Facebook Page. That includes anyone who has visited your Page, engaged with any post/ad, clicked on any call-to-action on your Page, sent a message to your Page or saved your Page or any post.

Follow the process as above by going to your Audiences tab in Facebook Ads Manager. Select Engagement and then Facebook Page. Select the Page that you'd like to use to pull the data and name your audiences. It's that easy!

#5: Display Advertising Retargeting

And the final method for Retargeting is outside Facebook. It's using display advertising. These are the banner ads you see when you are on any website across the web, say Huffington Post or Inc.com.

Create banner ads in different sizes with the same messaging I mentioned for Facebook ads earlier in this chapter. Be softer and not sales-y.

You can set up these retargeting banner ads within the Google Display Network, or with retargeting platforms such as Adroll or Retargeter. They are all easy to use and you can find instructions on how to set up these campaigns for each specific platform once you sign up. Again, keep your budgets to five to ten dollars per day and you will get amazing results!

Analytics

Keep in mind as you run your ads, whether it's on Facebook or using display advertising, check your analytics. You might want to update your ads once the performance starts to wane.

Here are the analytics to review when running Retargeting campaigns:

- Impressions – an ad is viewed once by a web visitor or displayed once on a web page. For retargeting your impressions will be relatively small because you are only retargeting traffic that has already engaged with your site or social media.

- Clicks – the number of click actions taken by a user. You want to keep an eye on this metric because if you are seeing low clicks then your audiences are not engaging with your ad. To improve on retargeting clicks, test out different ad designs.
- Click through rate – the percentage of times people saw your ad and clicked on the ad. The metric is clicks divided by impressions. The average click through rate for retargeting ads is about 2-5%. If your metrics are lower then improve your ad design.
- CPM – cost per thousand impressions. In paid media, the pricing is either by CPM or cost per click (CPC). Since CPMs are based on an auction model, retargeting CPMs in the US vary but in the range of $10 - $25.
- CPC – cost per click. CPCs are also based on an auction model, and this varies also by industry but the average retargeting CPCs are $0.25 - $10.
- CPA – cost per acquisition. This metric is the number of conversions divided by your total spend. This extremely varied based on your vertical. For B2C (business to consumer) models it can be $1 - $100. But for B2B (business to business) models it can be $100 to over a thousand dollars, depending on the price point of the product/service.
- Budget – the daily spend. For retargeting campaigns, start off with $5-10 per day.

Your Turn

A retargeting strategy will allow you to further engage with your prospects. And an engaged prospect is a lot more likely to purchase your product or services. Retargeting allows you to utilize the whole framework for extra effect. In a way, it's like doubling the results for your work.

You will set up your retargeting campaign in Days 57-60 (Week 9). And you are now done setting up your digital marketing framework! And you are ready to turn on all your campaigns!

Great job! If you implement the strategies and set up your campaigns as discussed in the book, you will see growth in your business!

This framework has taken me years to perfect but I wanted to share it with entrepreneurs. Being an entrepreneur is not easy but having this digital framework to follow will make your entrepreneurial journey much more effortless. This book is like having an easily accessible digital marketing advisor to lead the way.

Resources

Facebook Pixel Guide for WordPress, SquareSpace and Shopify — https://jeanginzburg.com/fbpixel
Google Display Network — https://goo.gl/8hUpCX
Adroll — https://goo.gl/MhXtHn
Retargeter — https://goo.gl/9gZb1d

Next Steps

This is the framework I use to double and even triple my clients' businesses. Now it's your turn! Take all that you have learned from this book and apply it to your business. Don't get overwhelmed. Take one chapter at a time. Test out and tweak the strategy. Not everything will work the first time.

If you enjoyed the content in this book, then I encourage you to take the next step! I am releasing a digital course in 2018. The course covers all the topics in this book, but in much greater depth. There is only so much you can write in a book. With the digital course, you will have access to videos, audios, diagrams and worksheets. And not only that, you will also have access to me! As part of the course, I will be leading a private group where I help you create and implement your strategies and campaigns.

To learn more about how to use digital marketing strategies to grow your businesses, then go here https://jeanginzburg.com/course. We are going to cover digital marketing topics including:

- Finding your ideal customer
- Creating the right messaging for your brand
- Formulating your products to engage with your prospects
- The #1 strategy for creating captivating content
- Using that content to engage with over 2 billion users using Facebook ads
- Bringing in those users to your marketing automation funnel and nurturing them over time so they will eventually know, trust and like your products and your brand. And more importantly buy your product or services

I have used this strategy with my current and previous clients to grow their businesses! This isn't just some theory, this has worked!

And it has tripled some of my clients' businesses to allow them to become successful entrepreneurs!

Sign up today (https://jeanginzburg.com/course) and once the digital course is live, I will be sure to send you a message.

I look forward to serving you and your digital marketing needs!

About the Author

Jean Ginzburg is a serial entrepreneur, and digital sales and marketing expert with more than 10 years of industry expertise helping companies scale revenue, optimize sales and marketing processes and improve productivity. Her strategies have simplified and automated marketing for over 2,000 small businesses, authors, experts, speakers, coaches and consultants in more than 10 countries. Jean has consulted with celebrity clients and bestselling authors. Jean is also the CEO of Ginball Digital Marketing. Ginball's clients range from brand name Fortune 500 companies to innovative start-ups. Her mission is to triple 5000 businesses in the next 10 years.

Jean's digital industry specializations include the following:
- Full funnel marketing strategy
- Facebook Advertising
- Customer avatar development
- Sales and Marketing Automation
- Social Media
- Email Marketing
- Product strategy
- Content strategy
- Retargeting
- Analytics

Jean has been featured in Forbes.com and the Huffington Post. Additionally, she has been a guest speaker on numerous podcasts including the B2B Growth Show, Brandcasting You and The Inspired Daily Grind Podcast.

Links to Social Media and Websites

Video Blog: **Marketing Success in 10 Minutes or Less**:
https://www.youtube.com/jeanginzburg
YouTube: https://www.youtube.com/jeanginzburg
Facebook: https://www.facebook.com/jeanginzburg
Twitter: https://twitter.com/jeanginzburg
Snapchat: https://www.snapchat.com/add/jeanginzburg
LinkedIn: https://www.LinkedIn.com/in/jeanginzburg
Blog: https://jeanginzburg.com/blog

Amazon Author Page:
https://www.amazon.com/author/jeanginzburg

Hire Jean to Speak at Your Event!

Book Jean Ginzburg as your Keynote Speaker and You're Guaranteed to Make Your Event Highly Entertaining and Unforgettable!

For over a decade, Jean Ginzburg has been educating, entertaining and helping entrepreneurs, authors, experts, speakers, consultants and coaches build and grow their businesses with online video, social media, paid social and product creation strategies.

Her origin story includes immigrating from Russia at the age of eight, growing up in a diverse neighborhood in Chicago, creating and failing at several businesses and finally creating a business that has grown leaps and bounds and in turn, helping her clients grow their businesses—several businesses to seven+ figures. She has diverse experience in many verticals and industries including digital courses, e-learning, physical products and SaaS (Software as a Service) solutions.

Her unique style inspires, empowers and entertains audiences while giving them the tools and strategies they need and want to get seen and heard, build and grow successful sustainable brands and businesses.

For more info, visit https://www.JeanGinzburg.com/speaking

One Last Thing

If you enjoyed this book or found it useful I'd be very grateful if you'd post a short review on Amazon. Your support really does make a difference and I read all the reviews personally so I can get your feedback and make this book even better.

If you'd like to leave a review then all you need to do is click the review link on this book's page on Amazon here:
http://amzn.to/2w8AZeV

Thanks again for your support!

Made in the USA
Las Vegas, NV
22 December 2020